ADVANTEE®

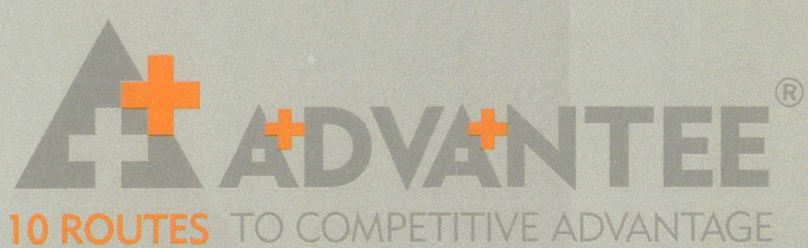

10 ROUTES TO COMPETITIVE ADVANTAGE

ADVANTEE®
10 ROUTES TO COMPETITIVE ADVANTAGE

	INTRODUCTION	Page 3
1	**PEOPLE**	Page 8
2	**PROCUREMENT**	Page 14
3	**METHOD**	Page 21
4	**DESIGN**	Page 26
5	**TECHNOLOGY**	Page 31
6	**IMPROVEMENT**	Page 36
7	**LOCATION**	Page 40
8	**SERVICE**	Page 44
9	**BRAND**	Page 48
10	**YOU**	Page 52

INTRODUCTION.

Having spent 35 years, working in businesses from very diverse sectors, a profile is built up on activity within each organisation. Some activity is productive, some activity non productive. The study of this activity first hand is what you will find in the following pages. It is intended to tease the reader into thinking how improvements can be made in their organisation. Most improvements might seem like common sense, but I have yet to see a book that explains what common sense is.

The 10 routes to competitive advantage give 10 clear topics for the business owner to focus on. Maximising output whilst minimising input in each of the 10 routes will result in creating efficiency gains without which, no business can be truly competitive.

INTRODUCTION

How the results affect your business is a question that only the market can answer. Why are some businesses returning 20% profits and others 10% in the same industry? They make similar products, sell to similar customers and yet operate in different ways. The difference is that the 20% profit business has learned to become efficient at what it does. It achieves more for less. It sells more for less and somehow remains competitive in the market place.

A common denominator is usually the elimination of waste. Not what goes in the skip round the back but the elimination of wasted time, resources, materials and anything else that does not add value in the eyes of the customer.

INTRODUCTION

Involvement with any external consultancy can be worthwhile only if the business owner can be brutally honest and divulge sensitive information to someone who may be a total stranger. This relationship takes time to nurture and honesty is not always forthcoming. Self diagnosis using the 10 routes to competitive advantage is the starting point and will highlight those areas of your business in most need of attention, quickly and inexpensively.

Improvement academics will give you the long hand, and almost scientifically critical theory which has been seen to work in large global businesses. Small businesses can't afford the luxury of consultants to go through the company, see what is wrong, offer a solution and get paid for a report that too often sits on the bookshelf because nobody has time to read it.

INTRODUCTION

For the small business operator, academia is not even on the horizon. Self diagnosis is not ideal, as any general practitioner will tell you. However, even in the medical arena, self diagnosis exists and has been seen to be successful in detecting early signs of possible health problems, hence the use of the 10 routes as a tool to use for self diagnosis.

Who does the diagnosis within the business is down to the business owner. What motivates this is the desire to do better, be more competitive, win that big order and be seen to champion best practice from all angles. The two quotes that underpin the 10 routes are etched in tablets of stone to remind the reader what this is all about. Ignorance is no reason for failure.

Colin V. Holmes © 2009

INTRODUCTION

> "It is not necessary to change, business survival is not mandatory."
> — W. Edwards Deming

> "Challenge everything, assume nothing and continuously improve."
> — Colin V. Holmes

PEOPLE

1 PEOPLE

People are the basis of the value adding process. Everyone must add value for the benefit of the customer.

Challenge the current use of labour within your organisation. Eliminate all non value adding activity.

Ensure everyone in your organisation has a customer focus. Is everybody adding value for the customers benefit.

Are the right people doing the right things for the benefit of the customer. Track the customer journey through your business and see where people are touched.

Question everything anybody does that doesn't add value to the customer. In the context of the objectives of the business, does everyone know what they should and should not be doing

PEOPLE

EXAMPLE 1

A craft jeweller making precious metal broaches used to cut the blanks out by hand from a sheet of raw material. This took 2 days per week to achieve. 5 miles down the road was a metal fabricating workshop with a CNC controlled laser profiling machine with spare capacity. Approaching the company, the blank shapes were scanned in and duly cut from the sheet blank with extreme precision in 30 minutes. Saving the jeweller 2 days of workshop time to work on other things.

PEOPLE

EXAMPLE 2

A family roofing business relied on accurate quotations for continuity of work. The quotes were all done manually from established costings sheets and transferred to a word document for presentation to the client. The managing director did all the quotes as it was only he who knew the costs of materials and the technical requirements of each different type of roof specification ie a stone flagged roof per square metre was different to a tiled roof and a slate roof and vice versa.

A spreadsheet was devised which took all the cost data for each generic roof and allowed a non skilled person to enter the square metreage of roof and let the spreadsheet calculate the costs including labour, wastage and contingency. This resulted in saving the MD 2 days per week to look at other new enquiries and more importantly reduced the time from site visit to quotation to the client.

PEOPLE

EXAMPLE 3

Sitting in a production directors office opposite a window overlooking the factory yard, a man was seen to walk from one factory building to another. Half an hour later, the same man returned across the yard and back into the original building. Not wishing to get the man into trouble, he was asked why he went to the other building. To borrow some tools he replied as his had been lost or stolen. The man was too afraid to report this to management and thought that borrowing tools was a better option. Eventually the tools were replaced and an open policy introduced for reporting faults/improvements etc to management. Morale and output improved immediately.

PEOPLE

In today's business climate, people don't have the luxury of lots of time to do things. To some degree we are all "time starved"©. Ecommerce has shown that customer expectation has changed. The customer journey has changed and ultimately the supply of goods and services has to change also.

People drive change when allowed to do so. Management of change within the context of people within your organisation is the way forward.

PROCUREMENT

2 PROCUREMENT

Procurement is the process of bringing into your organisation, that which does not already exist in it.

It can be raw materials, equipment, services.

- Eliminate all non value adding material.
- Challenge the fitness for purpose of all material.
- Ensure stock level is appropriate to business requirements.
- Everybody is everybody's customer.

PROCUREMENT

EXAMPLE 1

A catering equipment manufacturer had been making the same products for 20 years. No one questioned the specification. Over time, materials become cheaper/more expensive. Side panels on large ranges were made of thick gauge stainless steel. Now not a structural component, they were aesthetic and could be fabricated using thinner gauge materials with no detriment to the product. This company made six figure cost savings on materials.

PROCUREMENT

EXAMPLE 2

A contract furniture manufacturer was challenged with producing an interior for a chain of a high street business in the financial sector. The designers specified prime solid ash timber for a component in the interior which was purely decorative. To supply the whole contract with this one component meant several kilometres of the moulding needed to be supplied not including the 50% wastage whilst machining the component. The design was changed to a veneer wrapped MDF profile which was mechanically more stable and 75% cheaper with no detriment to the effect in the interior.

PROCUREMENT

EXAMPLE 3

A factory owner wondered how he was going to raise the finance to build the 10,000 square foot extension he needed for his factory. The extension was needed for expansion and to house new machinery. In actual fact, the owner thought his premises were full to capacity but because he was so close to it, he couldn't see the reality. Every space in the factory was crammed with stock, old raw materials, redundant machinery and scrap.

He didn't need a factory extension; he needed to manage the existing workspace. After consultation, he developed his supplier relationships to hold stock at their premises on consignment until needed for production. Old machinery and goods were disposed of and all unnecessary items removed, releasing space internally for the expansion and new machinery.

PROCUREMENT

EXAMPLE 4

NASA spent $1 million developing a pen to take into space……. The Russians took a pencil.

Whether this is true or not, it demonstrates the issue of fitness for purpose. If a pencil will do the job, use a pencil. Why re invent the wheel? If floating micro particulate will jeopordise the mission, design it out. Again, the issue here is fitness for purpose.

The quote " challenge everything, assume nothing and continuously improve " could almost have been written to underpin procurement.

PROCUREMENT

Whether you make a product or deliver a service, challenge everything leaves no stone unturned. Ask yourself:

"why is this the way it is?"

"why do we do this?"

"why do we need this?"

"why do we use this?"

"why do we need stock of this?"

"why do we use this supplier?"

Assume nothing. Not even the most trivial of issues. Going through this process thoroughly gives peace of mind. Even if nothing changes, you have the knowledge and confidence that all is well with your own procurement.

METHOD 3

3 METHOD

Method is anything your organisation does to achieve your output.

- Eliminate all non value adding processes.
- Challenge and process map all current procedures and methods.
- Ask to what end does this process add value.

METHOD

EXAMPLE 1

A woodwork factory made components for other manufacturers. Frequently parts were machined only to be rejected by inspection for poor quality material. Quality is the responsibility of everyone and time and effort should not be wasted on processing that which should not be processed in the first place.

EXAMPLE 2

A factory using CNC cutting machinery trusted the operator to programme the machine. Under observation, the cutting head travelled at the same speed for traversing as it did for cutting. No fault of the operator as he did not know any different. Challenging everything means do not take anything for granted. The traverse speed was maximised saving over a minute per cycle and over 2 hours per day. Therefore creating extra capacity on the machine.

METHOD

EXAMPLE 3

An open plan office had expanded in the way most do. New staff come in, desks are moved around etc. No one queried the fact that the main filing cabinets for the largest team were now over 5 metres away necessitating a lot of walking to access the files. The cabinets were eventually moved to where they were actually needed resulting in increased motivation for the staff to file things where they should be.

EXAMPLE 4

A fish and chip shop is perceived as fast food, but in some shops, the person serving is the same person collecting the order, wrapping and taking the money, resulting in queues, dissatisfied customers especially those who happen to be behind the person picking up the lunchtime order for the local factory. One fish and chip shop has studied this and designed a service level never seen before. One person takes the order, another

METHOD

person collates the order and wraps it whilst another person has already rung the order into the till and is taking the money. This increases the throughput with minimal waiting time and plenty of happy repeat customers combined with great quality food. The extra staff are part time (peak time) and the overhead is easily covered by the massive increase in turnover.

Methods are easily observed. Over time, custom and practice can blind people into monotonous routine. Challenge these routines and ask, " why do we do this?".

Ideally, each operation, task, procedure should add value otherwise why do it. The customer won't pay for something they don't get. Are you paying for an overhead that has no benefit to the customer? At least question the reason for this and be happy with the answer you give.

DESIGN

4 DESIGN

Design is the process by which value is added to raw materials, processes and services.

Design out all non value adding elements, processes and cost.

Give your customer more value for least cost.

Influence your customers' journey.

Walk in the customers shoes.

DESIGN

EXAMPLE 1

A retailer has designed a service so that instead of carrying armfuls of goods around whilst shopping, you receive a ticket for your goods at each section. When you finish shopping, you take your tickets to the till and miraculously, all your items are there, ready and waiting for payment. Total customer satisfaction.

EXAMPLE 2

A budget airline does not have reclining seats, window blinds, seat pockets and headrest covers. They have been designed out to reduce cost by making the cleaning easier and passing cost savings onto the customer. Saving time cleaning means that the aircraft can be turned around quicker, giving more flights per day with the same number of aircraft to more passengers. Simple.

DESIGN

EXAMPLE 3

You drive to a business and the car parking space nearest the door has a number plate screwed to the wall saying **Managing Director.** What message does that give to customers'. It sort of says that you are more important than them. Let customers park nearest the door.

DESIGN

EXAMPLE 4

A recent hotel visit highlighted how easy it is to get things wrong. On the outside things look good, but when it comes to functionality, it doesn't work. The wardrobe door won't open fully because of the large chair placed in front of it. The TV is partially obscured by a fan placed because of poor ventilation. The shower curtain over the bath acts like cling film because the specific bath is a narrow one. Walk in the customers shoes and don't give him a reason to complain. Design the customers journey.

This isn't an easy one. Changes to design might not be an option due to certain circumstances. The trick here is to walk in the customers shoes. What is it about what you do that makes the customer come back? Find this out and do more of it.

EXPLOIT TECHNOLOGY

5

TECHNOLOGY

5 EXPLOIT TECHNOLOGY

Technology constantly evolves. Awareness of new technology provokes the question of whether to use it or not.

Could technology replace labour?

Could technology add value to your customer's journey?

Challenge the use of latest technology at every stage.

TECHNOLOGY

EXAMPLE 1

Corner shop bar code reader. People now are accustomed to fast accurate service as demonstrated by large supermarkets. Using technology in small retailers gives them the benefit of accurate stock control, promotional activity options and reduced queues.

EXAMPLE 2

An online bookstore became famous for literally opening a bookstore in every street in the world backed up by a warehousing service second to none. The use of the website as a silent salesman reduces overheads, and integrated with email becomes a comprehensive accurate means of communicating with customers.

TECHNOLOGY

EXAMPLE 3

A new branded coffee bar had to create a massive first impression due to major competition from the big boys. Researching the market for quality bean to cup machines, he emerged with one which gave the customer the high quality demanded within 22 seconds. Throughput is fast and minimises waiting time. Customer satisfaction is very high therefore creating brand loyalty which in turn can be rewarded through the interactive till and point of sale equipment.

EXAMPLE 4

Budget airlines use technology to keep prices low with online booking, online check in, ticket less travel, minimal baggage handling and online payment. All integrated to give a customer experience in parallel with the price he wants to pay.

TECHNOLOGY

EXAMPLE 5

Be the first window cleaner to set up direct debits for customers who do not have ready cash on a Friday night. Carrying less cash around reduces the risk of becoming a mugging victim.

Exploiting technology only gives competitive advantage if the technology itself is relevant to the business. It is no good investing in a website if you don't need one.

The question " what is relevant technology?", is answered by your customer. If there is no impact on the customer in terms of price, service or deliverables then it isn't relevant.

CONTINUOUS IMPROVEMENT

6

6 CONTINUOUS IMPROVEMENT

Continuous improvement should be routine and embedded in the organisations culture.

- Challenge everything everyday.
- Ask why do we do this.
- Ask the customer.
- Constantly improve the product, process, material, service.

CONTINUOUS IMPROVEMENT

EXAMPLE 1

The aspect of continuous improvement is most visible in everyday products: the PC, mobile phones, microwaves, laser technology, optical fibre data transmission, flat screen TV's, Formula 1 etc. The common element in successful improvement is change management or the management of change.

EXAMPLE 2

A football team not performing would not cut back on training, they would do more training. When your business doesn't perform, do you cut back on training? People need development too.

CONTINUOUS IMPROVEMENT

EXAMPLE 3

Continuous improvement in all 10 routes to competitive advantage maximises your companies chances of success. Change for the sake of change is a waste of time.

Each of the 10 routes can be used individually as a focus for continuous improvement. In the same way that continuous personal development increases your own knowledge and performance, continuous improvement in all areas of your business will increase the performance of it.

How much time do you spend working in the business when you should be working on it?. Do you only do things when your customer or competitor forces you to?.

LOCATION 7

7 LOCATION

The location of your organisation can have an effect on your relationship with customers. Location should be exploited for the benefit of the customer and the organisation.

Assess the location of your organisation in relation to your customer.

Walk your customers' journey.

Assess the relevance of location with business type.

LOCATION

EXAMPLE 1

A business is located highly visible on a major ring road with 20,000 vehicles a day passing by. The sign on the building visible to the road does not say what the business does. How many more customers could be captured if the messaging from the sign explained what the business did?

EXAMPLE 2

Take advantage of a captive audience. Ask the customer what they want. Businesses nearby may not be aware of what you do and as importantly, you may not be aware of what they do.

LOCATION

EXAMPLE 3

Understand the limits of your location. Parking, signage etc all contribute to the experience of your customers.

The phrase location, location, location usually relates to residential property. Used in the context of business, raises questions about the relevance of location with your business type or customer.

As long as you have maximised the potential of your location, or in auditing it, you are aware of any limitations, then you can be confident about its impact on your business and take action accordingly.

SERVICE

SERVICE

8 SERVICE

Service is the manner in which you engage business with anyone. Customers, suppliers, competitors and staff expect consistency and professionalism.

ASSUME NOTHING.

CHALLENGE EVERYTHING.

TEST IT YOURSELF.

SERVICE

EXAMPLE 1

Service is the experience your customer enjoys as a result of intervention with your business. Give your customer good service and chances are they will come back. Give your customer bad service and chances are you will have lost them for good.

Consistency of service is paramount. Don't give the customer a reason not to come back. Refer to the Design summary No. 4. You can design a service level to be higher than your competitors or one more appropriate to your customers requirements.

Service is everything you do, how you do it, present yourself, answer the phone, relate to colleagues, turn off the lights.

SERVICE

What your customer see's is not necessarily what you see, and if you don't test your own service, you may never know what's wrong with it. Complacency can breed over years and customers might not be honest with information on bad service and simply choose to go elsewhere. The secret shopper idea is simple, quick, informative and works.

BRAND

9 BRAND

Your brand is the statement you make of how you want people to perceive what it is that you do and how well you do it.

Be visible and memorable.

Give out appropriate messages.

Demonstrate brand values.

Secure intellectual property.

BRAND

EXAMPLE 1

Your brand is your silent salesman. It is there when you are not. It represents visibly your values, ethics, quality and services.

Why are some brands more memorable than others?

Most successful brands use one or two words in the brand name ie, Microsoft, Coca Cola, Nokia, McDonalds, American Express, Sony, Disney.

Can you enhance the brand with a qualifying statement or strapline?

Tesco – Every little helps.

Audi – Vorsprung Durch Technik.

Nike – Just do it.

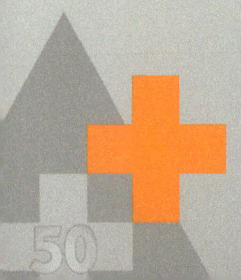

BRAND

Does your brand reflect the messages that your customers see?

It needs to be:

Memorable.

Demonstrate brand values.

High visibility.

Fitness for purpose. Reflecting the ethos of the business and not just a graphical representation of the business name.

Consistency is the essence of good branding. The brand design is no good if it is not represented consistently either in shape, size, proportion, colour or messaging.

Good brands become valuable over time and become instantly memorable by the fact that they have been represented consistently.

Ownership of brand name is vital and the only route to this is by owning the trade mark. Seek advice for intellectual property.

YOU

10

10 YOU

In order to maximise competitive advantage, the ultimate driver of change is the business owner. Management of change is key to successfully integrating the 10 routes to competitive advantage within your organisation.

> "IT IS NOT NECESSARY TO CHANGE, BUSINESS SURVIVAL IS NOT MANDATORY."
> W. EDWARDS DEMING

YOU

CULTURE
We've always done it like that. Why?

CAPACITY
Do you want bigger, better, more? When?

CURE
The management of change. How?

> "CHALLENGE EVERYTHING, ASSUME NOTHING AND CONTINUOUSLY IMPROVE."
> — COLIN V. HOLMES

CONTINUOUS IMPROVEMENT

CULTURE

The ultimate driver of change is the business owner. The culture of the business is driven by the business owner. If the business owner can't manage change, then complacency will prevail.

CAPACITY

Do you want the phone lines burning holes in your carpets with new customers needing servicing?

Do you want your business to be the envy of others especially your competitors?

CONTINUOUS IMPROVEMENT

CURE

The management of change to implement change.

The business owner, board of directors, management, employer, employee etc. everyone contributes. There is no dead wood.

If you are too busy to work on the business because you are too busy working in the business, then nothing will change.

Change management is imperitive. The management of change to implement change.

Colin V. Holmes © 2009

ADVANTEE.COM

Competitive advantage, online.

Further information and my blog are online to help you gain competitive advantage.

If you have questions or comments please contact me through the website.

THANK YOU

I hope this book helps you gain competitive advantage..

If you need to discuss your specific situation and would like my help in finding your route to competitive advantage, email me at colin@advantee.com

Colin V. Holmes

10 ROUTES TO COMPETITIVE ADVANTAGE

©2009 Colin V. Holmes

www.ingramcontent.com/pod-product-compliance
Lightning Source LLC
Chambersburg PA
CBHW041132200526
45172CB00018B/145